RAPPER'S DELIGHT
THE HIP HOP COOKBOOK

© 2014 Dokument Press & Inniss, Miller & Stadden
First edition, fourth printing
Printed in Poland 2016
ISBN 978-91-85639-70-0

Editors: Joseph Inniss, Ralph Miller and Peter Stadden
Text: Joseph Inniss and Ralph Miller
Graphic design: Peter Stadden

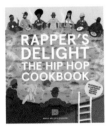

Cover illustration by Tom Clohosy Cole

Dokument Press
Box 773, 120 02 Årsta, Sweden
www.dokument.org
info@dokument.org

RAPPER'S DELIGHT
THE HIP HOP
COOKBOOK

INNISS, MILLER & STADDEN

S

INTRO

"HAVE YOU EVER WENT OVER A FRIEND'S HOUSE TO EAT AND THE FOOD JUST AIN'T NO GOOD? I MEAN THE MACARONI'S SOGGY, THE PEAS ARE MUSHED, AND THE CHICKEN TASTES LIKE WOOD."

Wonder Mike, Sugar Hill Gang – Rapper's Delight

Hip hop and food have a long and intertwined history. The genre has spawned many flavas and beefs, with numerous artists being inspired by culinary delights – A Tribe Called Quest's *'Ham 'N' Eggs'*, Nas's *'Fried Chicken'* and MF Doom's *'Mm.. Food'* album are just a few examples. Following on from that heritage this book pays tribute to the music, culture and creativity of hip hop.

Rapper's Delight: The Hip Hop Cookbook celebrates the many humorous parallels between food and hip hop. Featuring thirty recipes inspired by the most renowned hip hop artists of today and yesteryear, each of the book's dishes is accompanied by exclusive artworks created by our favourite illustrators.

We have tried to ensure this book caters for cooks of all abilities. Whilst some of the recipes are designed to be quick and easy to make, others require a little more skill and patience. Each recipe page includes a difficulty rating, outlining how hard it is to make. The *Beats Per Minute* (*B.P.M.*) gives a rough guide on how long the recipe takes to prepare and cook. All recipes are designed to serve four people.

On page 8 there is an *Equipment Matrix* so you know exactly what you'll need before you start cooking. We have also included an *Advanced Methods* section (from page 78) for those of you who are more confident in the kitchen or want to try something a little more tricky. There are also serving suggestions which will help you to turn your meal into a feast.

We hope this book will entertain and guide you in the kitchen, and possibly even expand your hip hop palette.

THE RAPPER'S DELIGHT TEAM
www.rappersdelightcookbook.com

CONTENTS

PREPARATION

8   Equipment Matrix

STARTERS

12   Public Enemiso Soup

14   Wu-Tang
          Clam Chowder

16   Mobb Leek &
          Potato Soup

18   MC Solaariac Soup

20   Prawn Carter Cocktail
          with Kanye Zest
          (That fish cray)

22   DM Eggs Benedict

24   MC Ham'n'Eggs

26   Ludacrispy Duck
          with Ho-Sin sauce

28   Method Lamb Koftas

30   MF SHROOM
          Burgers

MAINS

34   Notorious P.I.G.
          (Feat. 2Pak Choi)

36   Run DM Sea Bass

38   Grandmaster
          Flash-Fried Steak
          & The Furious Five
          Bean Salad

40   Lemon Sole
          of Mischief
          (Feat. The Phar-side
          of Wedges)

42   Snoop Stroganoff

44   Slick Ricotta Tart
          (Feat. Doug E
          Crème Fraîche)

46   Queen Labeefah

48   Pig Bun (Feat. Fat
          Joey Crackling)

50   A Pie Called Quest

52   N.W. Glazed Ham
          (Feat. Dr. Dravy)

DESSERTS

56	Eazy Eton Mess
58	M.O.Peach Cobbler
60	Nasty na'Nas & Custard
62	Busta Key Lime Pie
64	Tiramisu Elliott
66	KRS Buns
68	LL Cool Soufflé
70	Afrika Bambattered Pineapple Fritters & The Soul Sonic Sauce
72	Mousse Def (Feat. Talib Jelly)
74	The Sugar Hill Meringue

ADVANCED METHODS

78	Poaching a single egg
78	Using an egg poacher
79	Wrapped poaching method
79	Separating an egg
80	Gangstartar sauce
80	Accompanying vegetables
82	Colcannon mash
83	Creamed leeks
84	Slow cooking
85	Homemade custard

EXTENDED MIX

88	Recipe Index - Starters
90	Recipe Index - Mains
92	Recipe Index - Desserts
94	Rapper's Delight Mixtape
95	Outro

EQUIPMENT MATRIX

You gotta prep to keep your rep

Public Enemiso Soup

Wu-Tang Clam Chowder

Mobb Leek & Potato Soup

MC Solaariac Soup

Prawn Carter Cocktail with Kanye Zest (That fish cray)

DM Eggs Benedict

MC Ham'n'Eggs

Ludacrispy Duck with Ho-Sin sauce

Method Lamb Koftas

MF SHROOM Burgers

Notorious P.I.G. (Feat. 2Pak Choi)

Run DM Sea Bass

Grandmaster Flash-Fried Steak & the Furious Five bean salad

Lemon Sole of Mischief (Feat. the Phar-side of Wedges)

Snoop Stroganoff

Slick Ricotta Tart (Feat. Doug E crème fraîche)

Queen Labeefah

Pig Bun (Feat. Fat Joey Crackling)

A Pie Called Quest

N.W. Glazed Ham (Feat. Dr. Dravy)

Eazy Eton Mess

M.O.Peach Cobbler

Nasty na'Nas & Custard

Busta Key Lime Pie

Tiramisu Elliott

KRS Buns

LL Cool Soufflé

Afrika Bambattered Pineapple Fritters & the Soul Sonic Sauce

Mousse Def (Feat. Talib Jelly)

The Sugar Hill Meringue

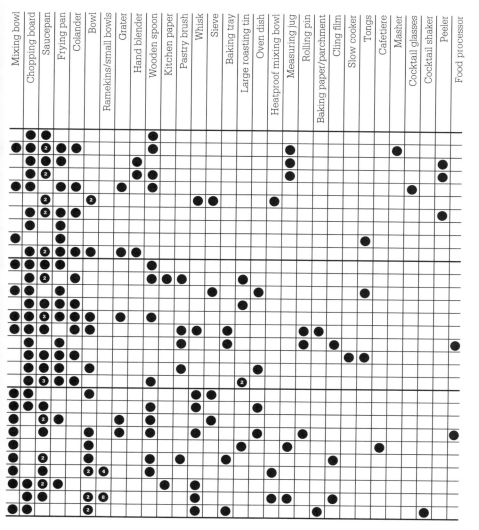

PREPARATION

STAR

PUBLIC ENEMISO SOUP
Check the Flava Flav

STARTERS

DIFFICULTY

DESCRIPTION
Thin traditional Japanese soup flavoured with distinctive miso (fermented soy beans).

B.P.M.
5 minutes preparation
10 minutes cooking

INGREDIENTS
75g / 3oz miso (comes as a sachet of purée)
3 green onions (scallions)
15g / half an oz nori seaweed
Half a block of firm silken tofu (approx. 150g / 5oz)
A dash of soy sauce
2 tablespoons of sesame oil
1 litre / 2 pints of water

NOTES
During the preparation of this soup, you should not allow the water to boil as this will destroy the flavour.

METHOD

1. Fill a saucepan with water. Place on the heat and bring to a boil. Reduce the heat to a slow simmer.
2. Peel and slice the green onions and set aside.
3. Finely slice the nori seaweed.
4. Slice the tofu into small cubes.
5. Add the nori seaweed to the water and continue to simmer for 6 minutes.
6. Reduce the heat to the lowest setting and add the miso.
7. Add the onions, tofu, sesame oil and a dash of soy sauce.
8. Stir until the miso is fully dissolved. This should take no longer than 3 minutes.
9. To serve, divide between the bowls and serve straight away.

WU-TANG CLAM CHOWDER

Ain't nuthin' to f*** with

DIFFICULTY

DESCRIPTION

Potatoes and fresh clams come together to make this thick rich and creamy dish.

B.P.M.

25 minutes preparation
45 minutes cooking

INGREDIENTS

1kg / 35oz fresh live clams
25g / 1oz dried dulse
(aka seaweed)
2 onions
1 leek
1 carrot
200g / 7oz streaky bacon
1 sprig of parsley
1 sprig of thyme
750ml / 1 and a half pints
of water
250ml / half a pint
of dry white wine
2 tablespoons of butter
1 vegetable stock cube
500g / 18oz potatoes
250ml / half a pint
of double cream

METHOD

1. Add the clams to a colander and wash under cold water.
2. Peel and finely slice one onion. Peel and slice the carrot and leek. Finely slice the dulse.
3. Add 500ml / 1 pint of water to a saucepan and bring to the boil. Add the dulse, onion, leek, carrot, parsley and thyme. Reduce the heat and leave to simmer for 10 minutes.
4. Add the white wine. Increase the heat, add the clams and cover with the saucepan lid. Allow the clams to cook in the liquid for 2 minutes or until they have all opened.
5. Place a colander over a mixing bowl. Strain the contents of the saucepan through the colander so the liquid is caught in the bowl. Set this liquid aside for later.
6. Pull the clams from their shells discarding all of the shells. Also discard the parsley and thyme. Return the shell-less clams, dulse and vegetables to the liquid in the bowl and set aside.
7. Add 250ml / half a pint of water to a saucepan and bring to a simmer. Crumble in the stock cube.
8. Slice the potatoes into cubes and add to the saucepan. Simmer gently for 8 minutes.
9. Peel and slice the remaining onion into small squares. Slice the bacon into small squares.
10. Add the butter to a frying pan and place on a low heat. Add the bacon and onion and fry for 6 minutes.
11. While the bacon is cooking, remove the potatoes from the heat and drain through the colander. Put half of the potatoes back into the saucepan and mash. Put the remaining cubes of potatoes back into the saucepan and stir into the mash using the wooden spoon.
12. Mix the fried bacon and onion into the mash. Add the clams, dulse, vegetables and liquid in the bowl and stir together.
13. Return the saucepan to a medium heat and bring to a simmer. Add the double cream and gently stir before serving.

MOBB LEEK & POTATO SOUP
Ain't such things as halfway cooks

STARTERS

DIFFICULTY

DESCRIPTION
A classic soup – leek, potato, cream, salt and pepper.

B.P.M.
10 minutes preparation
15 minutes cooking

INGREDIENTS
2 leeks
300g / 11oz potatoes
150g / 5oz smoked
streaky bacon
1 vegetable stock cube
30g / 1oz butter
300ml / half a pint
of double cream
750ml / 1 and a half pints
of water
A dash of olive oil
A pinch of black pepper

METHOD

1. Peel and slice the potatoes into cubes. Wash the leek and slice into thin rings.
2. Place a saucepan on the heat and add the butter.
When the butter has melted add the potatoes and leeks. Crumble the stock cube into the pan and stir thoroughly.
3. Put 750ml / 1 and half pints of water in a kettle and boil.
4. Add the boiling water to the potato, leek and stock in the saucepan. Simmer for 10 minutes.
5. While the potato and leeks are cooking, place the frying pan on a high heat. Add the olive oil and fry the bacon until golden brown.
6. Remove the saucepan from the heat and use the hand blender on the potato and leeks until smooth.
7. Add the double cream and stir thoroughly.
8. Divide the soup between bowls. Roughly slice the bacon and use to top as a garnish. Season with the black pepper.

MC SOLAARIAC SOUP

Soup with French roots

DIFFICULTY

DESCRIPTION

A hearty vegetable soup made with the distinctive earthy celeriac flavours.

B.P.M.

5 minutes preparation
25 minutes cooking

INGREDIENTS

350g / 12oz celeriac
150g / 5oz potato
30g / 1oz butter
1 leek
250ml / half a pint
of single cream
A bunch of chives
1 vegetable stock cube
600ml / 1 and a quarter
of a pint of water

METHOD

1. Slice the roots from the celeriac. Peel the celeriac and potatoes. Slice both into small cubes. Wash and slice the leek into thin rings.
2. Place a saucepan on the heat and melt the butter. Add the leek and cook for 3 minutes.
3. Add the celeriac, cover the saucepan with a lid and cook for a further 10 minutes.
4. Fill a second saucepan with the 600ml / 1 and a quarter of a pint of water and bring to the boil. Add the potato and crumble in the stock cube. Simmer for 6 minutes.
5. Add the celeriac and leek to the potatoes. Cover with the lid and leave to simmer for a further 6 minutes.
6. Stir in the cream, remove the saucepan from the heat and use the hand blender until the mix is smooth and even.
7. To serve, divide between the serving bowls. Cut short clippings of the chives over the soup.

PRAWN CARTER COCKTAIL WITH KANYE ZEST

That fish cray

DIFFICULTY

DESCRIPTION

Prawns and strips of crayfish with orange zest, cucumber, mayonnaise and a squeeze of lime.

B.P.M.

5 minutes preparation
4 minutes cooking
5 minutes cooling

INGREDIENTS

250g / 9oz prawns
with shells removed
250g / 9oz crayfish tails (or tiger prawns) with shells removed
1 lettuce
1 ripe avocado
1 orange
1 lime
Half a teaspoon of turmeric
A dash of olive oil
3 tablespoons of mayonnaise
1 teaspoon of Worcester sauce
1 teaspoon of Tabasco sauce

METHOD

1. Add the prawns and crayfish to a colander and rinse under cold water.

2. Grate the skin of an orange into a bowl to create a zest and set aside for later.

3. Slice the lettuce and peel and slice the avocado into cubes.

4. Place the lettuce and avocado into the cocktail glasses. Slice a lime in half and squeeze the lime juice over the lettuce and avocado.

5. Mix the mayonnaise, Worcester sauce, Tabasco sauce and turmeric in a mixing bowl using a wooden spoon.

6. Place a frying pan on the heat. Add the olive oil, orange zest, prawns and crayfish. Cook on a low heat for 4 minutes stirring continuously.

7. Take the prawns and crayfish off the heat and use a spoon to gently stir them into the mayonnaise mix.

8. Let this cool in the fridge for 5 minutes. Eschew* the mixture for this time.

9. To serve, top each of the cocktail glasses with the prawn and crayfish mix.

*No one knows what it means, but it's provocative.

DM EGGS BENEDICT

Eggs gon' give it to ya

STARTERS

DIFFICULTY

DESCRIPTION

An English muffin topped with a poached egg and a rich hollandaise sauce.

B.P.M.

15 minutes preparation
30 minutes cooking

INGREDIENTS

7 large free range eggs
4 toasting muffins
200g / 7oz unsalted butter
15g / half an oz
whole black peppercorns
A bunch of tarragon
Half a lemon
6 tablespoons of white
wine vinegar
1 tablespoon of malt vinegar
A pinch of salt
A pinch of black pepper

NOTES

You can prepare the hollandaise sauce the night before to save time when making your *DM Eggs* breakfast.

METHOD

For the hollandaise sauce

1. Place a saucepan on a high heat and add the white wine vinegar. Add the peppercorns and tarragon and boil until only half the liquid remains.
2. Strain the liquid through a sieve into a bowl and set the liquid aside for later. Discard the peppercorns and tarragon.
3. Separate the yolks from 3 eggs, setting aside the egg yolks in a bowl and discarding the egg whites.*
4. Fill a saucepan with water and bring to the boil. Reduce to a simmer and place the heatproof mixing bowl over the water.
5. Place another pan on a low heat and add the butter.
6. Add the egg yolks and the white wine vinegar (which was set aside earlier) to the heatproof bowl over the water. Ensure this is on a very low heat. Beat vigorously until it forms a golden airy foam.
7. One tablespoon at a time, whisk in the melted butter.

Continue to whisk and add the butter. When all mixed in, you should have a texture as thick as mayonnaise.
8. Squeeze the juices of half a lemon into the mixture. Add the salt and pepper and give a final stir. The sauce can be served hot or cold.

For the DM Eggs Benedict

1. Bring a saucepan of water to the boil and add the malt vinegar.
2. Poach each of the remaining 4 eggs in this pan for 3 minutes.**
3. Split each of the muffins and toast under a grill, turning once until golden brown on both sides.
4. To serve, spread some hollandaise sauce on each muffin, top with an egg and spoon over the remaining hollandaise sauce.

* See *Advanced Methods* p79.
** See *Advanced Methods* p78.

MC HAM'N'EGGS

Can't rush this

STARTERS

DIFFICULTY

DESCRIPTION

A delicious multi-layered treat – ham, eggs, fried potato and onion.

B.P.M.

2 minutes preparation
18 minutes cooking

INGREDIENTS

4 ham slices
4 eggs
4 bread slices (white or brown)
300g / 11oz potatoes
1 onion
50g / 2oz butter
A pinch of dried oregano
A pinch of salt

METHOD

1. Peel and slice the potatoes into small cubes. Place a saucepan on the heat and fill with water. Bring to the boil and add the potatoes. Leave to simmer for 6 minutes.

2. While the potatoes are cooking, place a glass over a slice of bread. Use a sharp knife to cut out a circle around the glass. Do this for each of the bread slices and the same for the ham slices.

3. Peel and finely slice the onions. Place a second saucepan on a low heat and add the butter. Add the onions and cook for 3 minutes.

4. Drain the potatoes in a colander and add to the saucepan with the onions. Continually stir the mix while you season with the salt and dried oregano. Leave on a low heat for 7 minutes, stirring occasionally.

5. Set the grill to medium and place the bread circles under to toast. Turn when they are golden brown and reduce the heat if necessary to avoid burning.

6. Melt the remaining butter into the frying pan. Crack all 4 eggs into the frying pan being careful that they don't run into each other. Fry the eggs for 2 minutes.

7. To serve, place the toasted circular bread in the centre of the plate. Top with the potato and onions. Carefully place the ham on top of the potato and onion before topping off with an egg.

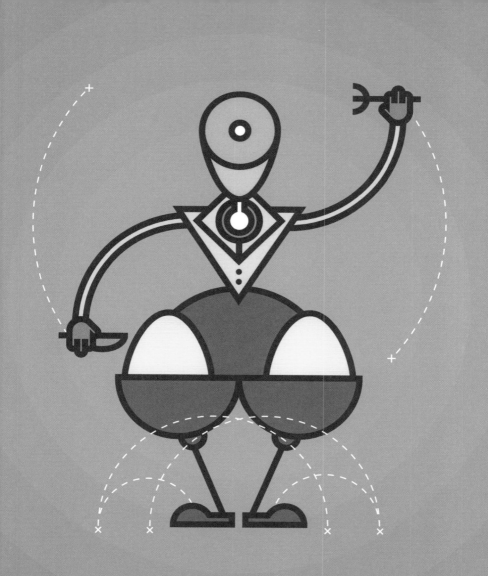

LUDACRISPY DUCK
With Ho-Sin sauce

DIFFICULTY

DESCRIPTION

Chinese-inspired finger food – crispy strips of duck, cucumber, celery, hoisin sauce and thin pancakes.

B.P.M.

10 minutes preparation
6 minutes cooking

INGREDIENTS

650g / 23oz duck breasts
Half a teaspoon
of Chinese five spice
2 tablespoons of sesame oil
1 teaspoon of sesame seeds
125ml / quarter of a pint
of hoisin sauce
8 ready-made Chinese-style
pancakes (or mini
flour tortillas)
1 celery
Half a cucumber
A bunch of spring onions
(approx. 100g / 4oz)

METHOD

1. Slice the roots from the spring onions, slice lengthways into thin strips and set aside.
2. Wash the celery and cucumber before slicing lengthways intro strips.
3. Slice the duck breast lengthways into thin strips. Place a frying pan on the heat and add the sesame oil. Add the duck and cook on a low heat for 2 minutes, turning continuously.
4. Add the five spice and continue to turn the duck for 4 minutes.
5. Add the hoisin sauce and sesame seeds and cook for a further minute.
6. Remove the pancakes from their packaging and place on a plate, heat in the microwave for 30 seconds (or in the oven as per the instructions on the pack).
7. To serve, transfer the duck, spring onions, celery and cucumber into separate serving bowls and allow everyone to create their own pancake wraps.

METHOD LAMB KOFTAS

M-e-t-h-o-d... lamb

DIFFICULTY

DESCRIPTION

Lamb kebabs made with chillies and fresh thyme and glazed with honey.

B.P.M.

5 minutes preparation
10 minutes cooking

INGREDIENTS

400g / 14oz lean lamb mince
1 teaspoon of ground cumin
1 teaspoon of olive oil
30g / 1oz chillies
3 sprigs of thyme
2 tablespoons of honey
A pinch of salt
A pinch of black pepper
Pack of mixed salad (optional)
Pitta breads (optional)
A dollop of natural
yoghurt (optional)

NOTES

You can either serve these koftas on skewers, or for a more substantial serving you can add pitta bread and salad.

METHOD

1. Place the lamb, cumin, chillies and thyme into a mixing bowl and stir the mix together.
2. Add the salt and pepper to season.
3. Using your hands divide the mix into 8 balls. If you are using skewers, slide the meat onto them now.
4. Place the frying pan on the heat and add the olive oil.
5. Lay the lamb kebabs in the frying pan for 8 minutes, ensuring the meat is turned regularly.
6. Remove the frying pan from the heat and glaze the meat with the honey. Return the kebabs to the heat and turn a few more times to ensure they are evenly coated with the glaze before serving.
7. If you desire, toast a pitta bread, cut open and serve with a few leaves of mixed salad. You can also add a dollop of yoghurt.

MF SHROOM BURGERS
Super grill'em!

DIFFICULTY

DESCRIPTION

A mushroom and chickpea patty in a burger bun, garnished with cheese and pickled gherkin.

B.P.M.

15 minutes preparation
15 minutes cooking

INGREDIENTS

250g / 9oz chestnut mushrooms
A bunch of spring onions
(approx. 100g / 4oz)
2 garlic cloves
1 tablespoon of curry powder
400g / 14oz canned chickpeas
1 lime
4 bread rolls
2 tomatoes
A handful of rocket leaves
150g / 5oz cheddar cheese
A pinch of salt
2 tablespoons of olive oil
4 slices of pickled gherkin
(or cucumber)

METHOD

1. Finely slice the mushrooms, garlic and spring onions.
2. Place the saucepan on the heat and add the olive oil.
3. Cook the mushrooms, garlic, salt and spring onions for 8 minutes on a medium heat. While the mix is cooking add in the curry powder. Cut the lime in half and squeeze the juice of both halves over the contents of the saucepan. When cooked pour the contents of the saucepan into a mixing bowl.
4. Fill a second saucepan with water, cover with its lid and bring to the boil. Drain the water from the chickpeas can and pour the chickpeas into the saucepan. Simmer for 4 minutes.
5. Remove the saucepan containing the chickpeas from the heat and, using a colander, drain away the hot water. Return the chickpeas to the saucepan and using the hand blender roughly pulse the chickpeas. Do not blend too much as you want to retain some of the natural texture of the chickpeas.

6. Add the partially blended chickpeas to the mushroom mix and stir.
7. Using your hands shape this mix into 4 patties. Place the frying pan on the heat and cook the patties for 4 minutes on each side.
8. While the patties are cooking, grate the cheese into a bowl and slice the tomatoes.
9. Using the bread knife slice each of the bread rolls in half and place them on a plate. Lay the rocket leaves out in the bread buns and share out the sliced tomatoes.
10. Place a burger patty on the rocket and tomato bed. Sprinkle over the grated cheese. Add a sliced pickled gherkin and finish by replacing the top of the bread roll.

TOM J NEWELL

MA

NOTORIOUS P.I.G.

Feat. 2Pak Choi

MAINS

DIFFICULTY

DESCRIPTION

Pork medallions served with a pak choi coleslaw and boiled new potatoes.

B.P.M.

10 minutes preparation
15 minutes cooking

INGREDIENTS

12 pork medallions
3 pak choi (Chinese cabbage)
Half a red cabbage
600g / 21oz new potatoes
1 red onion
1 carrot
A bunch of spring onions
(approx. 100g / 4oz)
A bunch of mint leaves
A bunch of coriander
(leaves only)
75g / 3oz Japanese
pickled ginger
5 tablespoons of mayonnaise
1 tablespoon of olive oil
25g / 1oz butter
A pinch of salt
A pinch of black pepper

METHOD

1. Peel and finely slice the red onion. Trim the roots of the spring onions and finely slice. Wash and finely slice the red cabbage. Wash and finely slice the pak choi leaves. Tear the mint and coriander leaves. Wash and grate the carrot.

2. Add the red onion, spring onion, sliced cabbage, pak choi, mint, coriander and grated carrot to a mixing bowl.

3. Add the mayonnaise and pickled ginger to the mixing bowl and vigorously stir. This will form a coleslaw.

4. Place a saucepan on a high heat, fill with water and bring to the boil. Add the new potatoes and reduce to a simmer. Cook them in the saucepan for 10 minutes.

5. While the potatoes are cooking, place a frying pan on a medium heat. Add the olive oil and the pork medallions. Fry the medallions for 8 minutes, turning occasionally.

6. When the potatoes are cooked drain through a colander. Add a tablespoon of butter to the drained saucepan and place on a low heat so that the butter melts. Return the potatoes to the saucepan and stir so they are covered in butter. Add a pinch of salt and a pinch of black pepper.

7. To serve, place 3 pork medallions on each plate and add a heap of the coleslaw. Add a portion of the potatoes to each plate.

RUN DM SEA BASS

It's not that tricky

DIFFICULTY

DESCRIPTION

Sea bass baked in rock salt and served with boiled vegetables.

B.P.M.

5 minutes preparation
25 minutes cooking

INGREDIENTS

450g / 16oz sea bass
(pre-scaled and gutted)
or four fillets of sea bass
500g / 18oz coarse rock salt
4 sprigs of rosemary
Half a lemon
600g / 21oz new potatoes
200g / 7oz broccoli
200g / 7oz green beans
50g / 2oz butter

NOTES

This dish can be cooked with a whole sea bass or with sea bass fillets. If using a whole sea bass you can ask your fishmonger to scale and gut the fish for you.

METHOD

1. Lay out around half the salt to form a layer at the bottom of a large roasting tin. Ensure the fish is dry using kitchen paper. Place the sprigs of rosemary in the fish's body cavity, or if using fillets lay out over the flesh.
2. Lay the whole fish, or the fillets, on top of the salt layer, then cover the fish with the remaining salt. The fish should be encased in salt. Wet your hands and flick a little water over the salt.
3. Pre-heat the oven to 200°C / 400°F / Gas Mark 6.
4. Place the roasting tin in the centre of the oven and cook for 25 minutes.
5. While the fish is baking, you can prepare the vegetables. Wash the potatoes and set aside. Slice the broccoli into small trees and rinse the green beans under cold water.
6. After the fish has been cooking for 10 minutes, fill a saucepan with water and bring to the boil. Add the new potatoes and leave to cook for 10 minutes.

7. After a further 2 minutes place the broccoli and beans in a saucepan and cook for 7 minutes.
8. Slice the lemon into wedges and set aside.
9. When the fish is cooked, remove the roasting tin from the oven and gently break the salt crust with a knife. Using a pastry brush and a spoon remove the salt crystals from the fish (you may find it is easiest to remove the entire skin). Ensure the vast majority of the salt is removed. Carefully lift the fish from the salt base and place onto a serving board or plates. Discard the salt.
10. Squeeze a little juice from the lemon over the fish and place the lemon wedges on top.
11. Drain the vegetables, then the potatoes through the colander and lay them out on the plates. Slice the butter into small chunks and melt over the vegetables and potatoes.

MAINS

GRANDMASTER FLASH-FRIED STEAK
& the Furious Five bean salad

DIFFICULTY

DESCRIPTION
Super-hot fast cooking steak served with a furiously-fresh bean salad.

B.P.M.
20 minutes preparation
(can be left to marinate overnight)
5 minutes cooking

INGREDIENTS
4 beef steaks (approx. 200g / 7oz each)
1 lemon
1 lime
1 orange
4 tablespoons of rum
1 tablespoon of olive oil
1.2kg / 42oz tinned mixed bean salad (3 tins)
400g / 14oz tinned lentils (1 tin)
1 red onion
A bunch of mint
A bunch of coriander
A bunch of parsley
2 tablespoons of white wine vinegar
A pinch of salt and black pepper

METHOD

1. To prepare the steaks, place them into a flat dish. Slice the lemon, lime and orange into halves and squeeze their juices over the steaks. Add a tablespoon of rum (the rest of the rum will be used later) and the black pepper. Leave the steaks to marinate for at least 1 hour (but they can be cooked straight away).

2. Place a saucepan on a high heat. Fill with water and bring to the boil. Remove the lentils from the tin and add to the saucepan. Cook for 4 minutes before using a sieve to drain the water. Leaving the lentils in the sieve, rinse them under cold water to cool. Add these to a mixing bowl.

3. Put the mint, coriander, parsley and the white wine vinegar into a food processor and blend. Season with the salt and pepper. Add these to the mixing bowl.

4. Remove the mixed beans from the tins and drain through a sieve. Add to the mixing bowl.

5. Peel and finely slice the red onion and add to the mixing bowl.

6. Thoroughly mix all the ingredients and divide the salad between the plates.

7. Place a frying pan on a high heat and add the olive oil. Heat for one minute.

8. Add the steaks to the frying pan and quickly splash over the three tablespoons of rum. Swirl it around the frying pan for 10 seconds. If you are using a gas hob, with care, tilt the pan to meet the flames to allow the alcohol to ignite.

9. After 30 seconds flip the steaks over. After a further 30 seconds remove the pan from the heat and place the steaks on the plates alongside the salad and serve immediately. The steaks should be browned on the outside and red on the inside.

MAINS

LEMON SOLE OF MISCHIEF

With the Phar-side of wedges

MAINS

DIFFICULTY

DESCRIPTION

Fried lemon sole seasoned with ginger and chilli, served with wedges and homemade *Gangstartar sauce*.

B.P.M.

15 minutes preparation
50 minutes cooking

INGREDIENTS

4 lemon sole fillets
1 lemon
500g / 18oz potatoes
200g / 7oz butternut squash
200g / 7oz carrots
30g / 1oz ginger
50g / 2oz fresh chilli peppers
250ml / half a pint of olive oil
50g / 2oz salted butter

NOTES

You can use tartar sauce pre-made from your local supermarket or alternatively check out the *Advanced Methods* on p80 to make your own *Gangstartar sauce*.

METHOD

1. Leaving the skins on, slice the potatoes into thick wedges. Slice the carrots into batons similar in size to the potato wedges. Peel and slice the butternut squash into wedges that are again a similar size.
2. Pre-heat the oven to 200°C / 400°F / Gas Mark 6.
3. Pour two-thirds of the olive oil into the large roasting tin and place in the oven.
4. Bring a saucepan of water to the boil and add the potato wedges. Maintain a boil in the pan for 5 minutes before bringing the water down to a low simmer.
5. Now add the butternut squash and the carrots. Leave the saucepan to simmer on a low heat for a further 15 minutes before draining the water from the pan using a colander.
6. Take the large roasting tin out of the oven. Being careful of the hot oil, place the boiled potatoes, butternut squash and carrot wedges into the roasting tin and return to the oven.

7. Turning every 15 minutes, roast the wedges and batons for approximately 35 minutes.
8. While the wedges are roasting, finely slice the ginger and chilli peppers. Cut the lemon in half and set aside for later.
9. 5 minutes before the wedges are ready, heat the remaining third of the olive oil in a frying pan on a high heat. Add the ginger and chilli peppers and stir.
10. Place the fillets in the frying pan. After 2 minutes turn them over and add the butter to the frying pan. Cook for a further 2 minutes.
11. Remove the pan from the heat and wait for 30 seconds before squeezing the juice from the lemon over the fish. Move the frying pan about to prevent the juice burning.
12. Carefully remove the roasting tin from the oven and divide the wedges between the plates. Add the sole fillets, one on each of the plates, with a generous portion of *Gangstartar sauce*.

SNOOP STROGANOFF
Eat beef everyday

DIFFICULTY

DESCRIPTION

A ginger twist on a Russian dish, sautéed beef on a bed of potatoes.

B.P.M.

1 hour 15 minutes preparation
25 minutes cooking

INGREDIENTS

600g / 21oz beef steak
400g / 14oz fresh mushrooms
4 large potatoes
120ml / quarter of a pint of soy sauce
120ml / quarter of a pint of sherry
A clump of fresh ginger (enough to grate into 2 tablespoons)
1/2 tablespoon of caster sugar
1 garlic clove
1 and a half teaspoons of paprika
50g / 2oz butter
1 onion
150ml / one third of a pint of sour cream
2 tablespoons of olive oil
A pinch of salt
A pinch of black pepper

METHOD

1. Cut the beef into roughly 3 cm / 1 inch chunks.
2. Peel and slice the onion into small chunks. Slice the mushrooms into small chunks. Set both these aside.
3. Peel the skin from the ginger and grate 2 tablespoons of ginger. Peel and finely slice the garlic. Add the ginger, garlic, soy sauce, sherry and sugar to the mixing bowl and stir thoroughly. Add the steak chunks to the sauce and leave in the fridge to marinate for at least 1 hour.
4. While the steak is marinating, fill a saucepan with water, place on the heat and bring to the boil. Peel and slice the potatoes into small chunks and add to the saucepan. Reduce the water to a simmer and cook for 8 minutes.
5. Drain the potatoes through a colander and set aside in a bowl.
6. Rinse clean the colander and place over a second saucepan. Strain the marinated beef through the colander so the liquid is caught in the saucepan.
7. Place this saucepan on a low heat and bring to a simmer.
8. Place a frying pan on a medium heat and add the butter. Add the onions and mushrooms and cook for 4 minutes. Sprinkle the paprika over the beef. Add the beef chunks and cook for a further 3 minutes.
9. Pour the beef, onions and mushrooms into the second saucepan containing the marinade. Season with salt and black pepper and stir in the sour cream. Stir this thoroughly and leave on a low heat while you cook the potatoes.
10. Place the frying pan on a high heat and add the oil. Heat the oil for one minute. Add the potatoes and fry for 3 minutes on each side (or until golden brown all over). Season with salt and black pepper.
11. Lay out the potatoes on the serving plates and pour over the beef, onion and marinade.

SLICK RICOTTA TART
Feat. Doug E crème fraîche

MAINS

DIFFICULTY

DESCRIPTION
Spinach and ricotta cooked on a puff pastry base and topped with crème fraîche.

B.P.M.
20 minutes preparation
20 minutes cooking

INGREDIENTS
250g / 9oz ricotta cheese
250g / 9oz spinach
100g / 4oz parmesan cheese
100g / 4oz sun-blushed tomatoes
500g / 18oz puff pastry
50ml / one fifth of a pint
of olive oil
1 egg
Plain flour
(for dusting the surface)
A small knob of butter
(to grease the baking paper)
A pinch of black pepper
A pinch of salt
250g / 9oz crème fraîche

METHOD

1. Pre-heat the oven to 200°C / 400°F / Gas Mark 6.

2. Place a saucepan on a high heat and fill with water. Add a pinch of salt and bring to the boil. Fill a bowl with cold water.

3. To blanch the spinach, add it to the boiling water for 30 seconds then drain it through a colander. Place the drained spinach in the cold water and then drain through the colander again.

4. Slice the tomatoes and place in a mixing bowl with the ricotta. Grate the parmesan and add to the bowl. Add the blanched spinach, pour on the oil and stir thoroughly.

5. Lightly flour a surface and roll out the puff pastry into a rectangle. Using a knife, mark a smaller rectangle inside the puff pastry rectangle, taking care not to slice all the way through.

6. Crack an egg into a bowl and beat it. Brush the pastry with the beaten egg.

7. Grease a piece of baking paper with the butter and place on the baking tray.

Lay the pastry on the greased baking paper. Spread the spinach and cheese mixture evenly over the puff pastry within the smaller rectangle.

8. Bake the tart in the oven for 20 minutes.

9. Remove the baking tray from the oven and sprinkle with a pinch of black pepper.

10. Divide the tart into slices and pour over as much or as little crème fraîche as desired.

QUEEN LABEEFAH

All hail the Queen

MAINS

DIFFICULTY

DESCRIPTION

Beef Wellington made with a rich mushroom pâté.

B.P.M.

30 minutes preparation
30 minutes cooking
10 minutes cooling

INGREDIENTS

500g / 18oz beef fillet
1 tablespoon of olive oil
250g / 9oz mushrooms
1 sprig of thyme
12 slices prosciutto ham
500g / 18oz pack puff pastry
Plain flour (for dusting a surface)
1 egg
A pinch of salt
A pinch of black pepper

NOTES

This recipe is for *Queen Labeefah* only, however it goes perfectly with colcannon mash and creamed leeks as shown in the *Advanced Methods* on pages 82-83.

METHOD

1. Add the mushrooms, salt and pepper to a food processor and blend.
2. Place a frying pan on a high heat and add the olive oil. To sear the beef, add it to the pan and fry for 3 minutes, turning continually. Ensure all surfaces are browned, including the ends. Set the beef aside for later.
3. Place the frying pan back on the heat and add in the mushroom. Cook the mushroom for 4 minutes and add the sprig of thyme. Once it has become thicker and pâté-like, discard the thyme and remove from the heat.
4. Over a chopping board lay out a sheet of cling film. Lay out the prosciutto slices to form a layer over the cling film. Lay out the mushroom paste in the centre of the prosciutto. Place the beef fillet on top of the mushroom and prosciutto slices.
5. Roll the cling film so the prosciutto and mushroom encases the beef. Twist the ends of the cling film so all the ingredients remain within the

cylinder and place in the fridge for around 15 minutes.
6. Dust a surface with plain flour and roll out the pastry ensuring it is larger than the beef fillet.
7. Dust the baking tray with the plain flour. Unwrap the meat from the cling film and place at the centre of the pastry rectangle. Roll the pastry over the meat until the two edges meet. Fold the ends and press together to ensure the beef is encased. Trim and discard any excess pastry. Place the wellington into the centre of the baking tray.
8. Crack the eggs into a bowl and beat. Brush the pastry with the eggs and score the edges of the pastry to decorate. Sprinkle salt over the glazed pastry.
9. Heat the oven to 200°C / 400°F / Gas Mark 6 and cook for 30 minutes. Allow the wellington to stand for 10 minutes before serving in thick slices.

PIG BUN

Feat. Fat Joey Crackling

MAINS

DIFFICULTY

DESCRIPTION

A pulled pork burger in a bread bun served with salad and crackling.

B.P.M.

10 minutes preparation
8 hours cooking

INGREDIENTS

600g / 21oz pork shoulder
Pork skin (from the shoulder)
250ml / half a pint
of barbecue sauce
330ml / half a pint of beer
Half a head of iceberg lettuce
4 tomatoes
1 onion
4 bread rolls
330ml / half a pint of sunflower oil

NOTES

If you don't have access to a slow cooker you can cook the shoulder on a very low heat in a saucepan full of water, just be sure to check it doesn't boil dry.

METHOD

1. Place the pork shoulder in the slow cooker.* Pour in the whole bottle of beer. Top up the bowl with water to ensure the pork is submerged. Put the lid on, and set the slow cooker to high. Cook the shoulder for 8 hours.

2. Place a saucepan on a high heat, fill with water and bring to the boil. Cut the pork skin into 4 evenly sized squares. When the water starts to boil place the skin pieces into the saucepan and reduce to a low simmer. Cook for 1 and a half hours. Occasionally check the pan has not boiled dry.

3. Drain the water and set aside to cool in the fridge for 3 hours.

4. Turn on the oven on its lowest heat setting. Place the skins in the oven to dehydrate for 3 hours. Open the oven door occasionally to check on the skins.

5. Around 30 minutes before the pork in the slow cooker is finished, slice the tomatoes, finely slice the lettuce and

onions and mix these together on each of the plates.

6. Place a frying pan on a high heat and add the sunflower oil. Heat the oil until it is very hot. Carefully place the skins in the frying pan and fry for 5 minutes. Turn the skins using tongs and cook for another 5 minutes. The skins should be crisp and golden brown. Remove the crackling from the frying pan and distribute between the plates.

7. Turn off the slow cooker and use a colander to drain away the liquid. Return the pork to the slow cooker bowl and pour in the whole bottle of barbecue sauce. Pull the meat apart, into stringy strips, using two forks. Thoroughly stir the pork with the sauce.

8. Slice the buns in half, and add a serving of the pulled pork. Add to the plate along side the salad and skins.

* See *Advanced Methods* p84 for how to slow cook meat – old school style.

A PIE CALLED QUEST

Can I lick it...? No, you can't

MAINS

DIFFICULTY

DESCRIPTION

An appley beef pie Bonita would be proud of.

B.P.M.

15 minutes preparation
1 hour 20 minutes cooking

INGREDIENTS

800g / 28oz stewing steak
225g / 8oz ready-rolled shortcrust pastry
330ml / half a pint of cider
A pinch of plain flour
A pinch of salt
A pinch of black pepper
1 tablespoon of olive oil
2 onions
2 garlic cloves
1 sprig of parsley
1 sprig of thyme
1 beef stock cube
2 eggs
A small knob of butter
(to grease the oven dish)

METHOD

1. Slice the steak into cubes and season with salt and pepper and a pinch of plain flour.
2. Place a frying pan on a medium heat and add the oil. Add the steak and stir continuously. Fry for 3 minutes until the meat is evenly browned. Remove from the heat and set aside for later.
3. Place a saucepan on a high heat and add the cider. Bring to the boil and crumble in the beef stock cube.
4. Peel and slice the onions, slice the parsley and thyme leaves.
5. Add the onions, parsley, thyme and beef to the saucepan. Reduce to a very low heat and simmer gently for 20 minutes.
6. Pre-heat the oven to 190°C / 375°F / Gas Mark 5.
7. Grease the oven dish with the butter. Lay out the pastry into the oven dish. Ensure all sides are covered so that the pastry overhangs the edge of the dish. Cut a second piece of pastry to fit across the top of the dish and set aside.

8. Crack the eggs into a bowl and beat them. Brush the pastry with half the beaten eggs.
9. Pour the beef mixture into the pastry-lined oven dish. Cover the pie with the second piece of pastry. Press the edges together to seal. You can decorate the pie with any leftover trimmings of the pastry.
10. Use a knife to make a steam hole in the centre of the pie. Brush the remaining egg over the top of the pie.
11. Place the pie in the oven and cook for 1 hour.
12. Slice the pie with a knife and serve hot.

N.W. GLAZED HAM

Feat. Dr. Dravy

MAINS

DIFFICULTY

DESCRIPTION

A honey-glazed ham served
with roast potatoes and a
rich homemade gravy.

B.P.M.

10 minutes preparation
2 hours 30 minutes boiling
1 hour roasting

INGREDIENTS

750g / 26oz unsmoked
boneless gammon joint
1 cinnamon stick
1 teaspoon
of whole peppercorns
1 teaspoon of coriander seeds
2 bay leaves
20 – 25 whole cloves
200g / 7oz demerara sugar
4 tablespoons of white
wine vinegar
4 tablespoons of Madeira wine
250g / 9oz honey
1kg / 35oz potatoes
75g / 3oz goose fat
A dash of olive oil
1 onion

METHOD

1. Place the gammon in a
saucepan and cover with cold
water. Add the peppercorns,
cinnamon, coriander seeds and
bay leaves and bring to the boil.
When the water boils reduce to
a simmer for 2 hours, topping up
the water if necessary.
2. Using a colander, strain the
liquid into a second saucepan
and set aside for later. Place the
ham into a large roasting tin and
discard the colander's contents.
Score the fat in a criss-cross
pattern and stud with cloves.
3. Pre-heat the oven to 200°C /
400°F / Gas Mark 6.
4. Peel the potatoes and slice
into chunks. Place a saucepan
on a high heat and fill with
water. Bring to the boil and add
the potatoes. Cook for 5 minutes
then drain through a colander.
Return the potatoes to the
saucepan, add the flour and a
pinch of salt. Put the lid on the
saucepan and shake to roughen
the edges.
5. Pour the goose fat into the
roasting tin and place in oven.
After 5 minutes, carefully remove

the roasting tin and add the
potatoes. Return the roasting
tin to the oven and cook for 40
minutes, turning occasionally.
6. To make the glaze, place a
saucepan on a high heat and
pour in the Madeira, vinegar,
sugar and honey. After 7
minutes remove from the heat.
7. Pour half the glaze over the
ham and cook in the oven for
15 minutes.
8. Remove the ham from the
oven and pour over the rest of
the glaze. Cook for a further
35 minutes.
9. Remove the ham from the
oven and leave to stand while
you make the *Dr. Dravy*.
10. Peel and slice the onion. Place
a frying pan on a high heat. Add
the oil and sliced onion. After 5
minutes transfer the onions to the
saucepan containing the liquid
set aside earlier.
11. Place the saucepan on a high
heat, crumble in the stock cube
and stir thoroughly.
12. Carve the ham and serve
with the potatoes and the
Dr. Dravy.

DESS

EAZY ETON MESS
With pistol-whipped cream

DESSERTS

DIFFICULTY

DESCRIPTION
A British classic –
strawberries, meringue and
thick whipped cream.

B.P.M.
15 minutes preparation
5 minutes cooking

INGREDIENTS
4 meringue nests
(approx. 50g / 1 and half oz)
500g / 18oz fresh strawberries
300ml / half a pint
of double cream
1 tablespoon of strawberry jam
1 tablespoon of icing sugar
1 drop of vanilla essence

NOTES
You can either make the
Sugar Hill Meringue as
featured on p74, or buy
pre-made from your
local supermarket. You can
prepare these up to 4 hours
before serving.

METHOD

1. Remove any leaves from the strawberries, and set aside the
four best looking ones for decoration later.
2. Slice all of the remaining strawberries into quarters and place
in a bowl.
3. Sieve half a tablespoon of the icing sugar over the strawberries.
4. Add the double cream to a mixing bowl. Using a whisk,
vigorously whip the double cream until it thickens.
5. Break the meringues into pieces and add to the cream in the
mixing bowl. Add the jam, vanilla essence and sliced strawberries
to the mixing bowl and gently stir using a metal spoon.
6. Split the mix between serving bowls and top each with one of
the whole strawberries.
7. You can store these in the fridge until you are ready to
bring them to the table. To serve, using the sieve, dust half a
tablespoon of icing sugar over the bowls.

M.O.PEACH COBBLER
Eat up that, fool!

DIFFICULTY

DESCRIPTION

A cross between a cake and
a crumble – peaches covered
in batter.

B.P.M.

15 minutes preparation
1 hour 10 minutes cooking

INGREDIENTS

150g / 5oz peaches
200g / 7oz self-rising flour
350ml / three quarters
of a pint of milk
120g / 4oz butter
350g / 12oz caster sugar
120ml / quarter of a pint
of water
300ml / half a pint
of single cream

NOTES

If you can't find fresh peaches
in your local supermarket you
can also use tinned peaches.
If doing so, substitute the
water in the ingredients for
the syrup in the tin.

METHOD

1. Pre-heat the oven to 180°C / 350°F / Gas Mark 4.
2. Peel and slice the peaches and discard the stone. Place a
saucepan on a medium heat and add the water and mix in the
peaches and 200g / 7oz of the sugar. Bring the mixture to a boil
and then reduce to a simmer. After 10 minutes remove from the
heat and set aside.
3. Place the butter in an oven dish and melt in the oven.
4. In a mixing bowl, whisk the remaining 150g / 5oz of sugar, flour
and milk together. Ensure the mix is smooth and there are no lumps.
This will form your batter.
5. Pour the batter over the melted butter in the baking dish, but
do not stir it in. Add the peach and sugar mix, ensuring that its
evenly spread across the dish.
6. Place the oven dish back into the oven and bake for 1 hour.
During this time the batter should rise in the dish.
7. Divide into portions and serve in bowls with the single cream
to taste.

DESSERTS

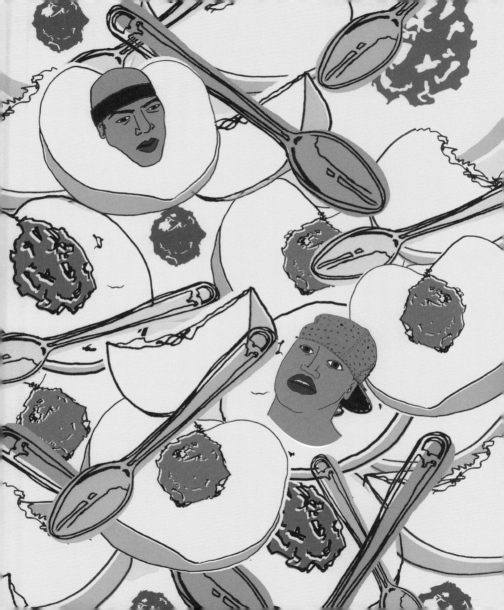

NASTY NA'NAS & CUSTARD

Made you cook

DESSERTS

DIFFICULTY

DESCRIPTION

Fresh bananas smothered in custard and topped with chilli chocolate.

B.P.M.

5 minutes preparation
15 minutes cooking

INGREDIENTS

4 bananas
1 tablespoon of icing sugar
100g / 4oz unsalted butter
100g / 4oz brown sugar
100ml / quarter of a pint of whipping cream
A dash of olive oil
600ml / 1 and a quarter of a pint of vanilla custard
A bar of chilli chocolate

NOTES

Refer to the *Advanced Methods* on p85 for instructions on how to make your own homemade custard.

METHOD

1. Peel the bananas and set aside.

2. Sieve the icing sugar into a mixing bowl.

3. Place a frying pan on a medium heat until hot. Add a dash of oil followed by the sieved icing sugar. Stir it together to create a dark brown caramel mixture.

4. Add the bananas and cook until golden brown. Remove the bananas from the frying pan and set aside.

5. Place a saucepan on a low heat, add the custard, stirring continuously. If the custard starts to thicken, remove the saucepan from the heat immediately.

6. After 2 minutes, place a second saucepan on a medium heat and add the butter, whipping cream and the brown sugar. Stir the mix together until it begins to bubble.

7. Add the browned bananas to the second saucepan. Cook them in the buttery sauce for a further 30 seconds.

8. Transfer the bananas to four serving bowls and serve with the custard. Grate the chilli chocolate over the top.

BUSTA KEY LIME PIE

Pass the Courvoisier

DIFFICULTY

DESCRIPTION

Key lime juice, egg yolks, Courvoisier and milk come together in a delicious pie.

B.P.M.

15 minutes preparation
25 minutes cooking
1 hour cooling

INGREDIENTS

300g / 11oz oaty biscuits
150g / 5oz butter
400g / 14oz tin
of condensed milk
3 medium eggs
4 limes (for zesting)
300ml / half a pint
of double cream
1 tablespoon of icing sugar
2 tablespoons of Courvoisier
(or other cognac)

NOTES

To crush the biscuits you can use a food processor, or bash them in a strong plastic bag using a rolling pin.

METHOD

1. Crack the eggs and separate the yolks* from the whites. Keep the yolks in a bowl and discard the egg whites.
2. Pre-heat the oven to 160°C / 320°F / Gas Mark 3.
3. Crush the biscuits into small crumbs, which will form the base of the pie.
4. Place a saucepan on a medium heat and add the butter. When the butter has melted take the saucepan off the heat, add the crushed biscuits and stir with a wooden spoon.
5. Press the butter and biscuit mix into the base of an oven dish.
6. Place this in the oven and bake for 10 minutes. Remove it and set aside to cool. Leave the oven on as you will soon be putting the full pie in again.
7. Grate the skin of 4 limes into a mixing bowl to create a zest. Squeeze the juice of the limes into the bowl and mix in 2 tablespoons of Courvoisier. Set aside a small amount of zest for decoration.

8. Whisk the egg yolks for a minute until they turn light. Add the condensed milk and whisk for 3 more minutes.
9. Add the zest, juice and Courvoisier to the egg yolk and condensed milk mix. Whisk again for a further 3 minutes. Pour this mix onto the cooled biscuit base. Return the pie back into the oven for a further 15 minutes. Cool for 1 hour.
10. When you are ready to serve, carefully remove the pie from the oven dish and place on a serving plate.
11. To decorate, softly whip together the cream and icing sugar in the mixing bowl. Spoon the cream onto the top of the pie and finish with a little extra lime zest.

* See *Advanced Methods* p79 for guidance on separating eggs.

TIRAMISU ELLIOTT

Open ya mouth, give you a taste

DIFFICULTY

DESCRIPTION

Savoiardi biscuits soaked
in espresso surrounded by
a cream and topped with
mascarpone cheese.

B.P.M.

30 minutes preparation
6 hours cooking

INGREDIENTS

125g / 4 and a half oz
savoiardi biscuits
500ml / 1 pint of water
4 tablespoons of strong
ground coffee
2 tablespoons amaretto liqueur
100g / 4oz mascarpone cheese
100g / 4oz vanilla custard
75ml / quarter of a pint
of whipped cream
2 chocolate flakes
(for decoration)
1 tablespoon of unsweetened
cocoa powder
1 teaspoon of instant
coffee powder
Coffee beans to garnish (optional)

METHOD

1. Add the ground coffee to a large cafetiere. Boil the water
in a kettle and pour into the cafetiere. Pour the coffee into a
measuring jug and stir in the amaretto.
2. Stir together the mascarpone and custard in mixing bowl.
Add the whipped cream and beat the mix thoroughly.
3. In a bowl mix together the cocoa and instant coffee powders.
4. For the first layer, place half the biscuits in the bottom of the
oven dish and drizzle with half the coffee and amaretto mix.
5. Spread half the mascarpone and custard mix over the
soaked biscuits and dust with half of the cocoa and coffee
powder mixture.
6. One at a time, dip the remaining biscuits in the rest of the
coffee and amaretto mix and lay out on top to form another layer.
7. Place the remaining mascarpone mix on top and dust with
remaining cocoa and coffee powder.
8. Crumble the flakes of chocolate and sprinkle over the top.
Decorate with coffee beans if you desire.
9. Chill the tiramisu for 6 hours to let it set. Once ready slice into
portions and serve on a plate.

KRS BUNS

It's the sound of the yeast

DESSERTS

DIFFICULTY

DESCRIPTION

Sweet white bread buns made with fresh yeast and topped with icing and a glacé cherry.

B.P.M.

15 minutes preparation
2 hours rising
30 minutes cooking

INGREDIENTS

450g /16oz strong white bread flour
150ml / third of a pint of milk
75g / 3oz butter
100g / 4oz soft light brown sugar
100g / 4oz mixed dried fruit
50g / 2oz honey
7g / quarter of an oz sachet of fast action bread yeast
2 medium eggs
1 teaspoon of ground cinnamon
A dusting of plain flour (for kneading the dough)
2 tablespoons of icing sugar
12 glacé cherries
A pinch of salt

METHOD

1. Add the bread flour to a mixing bowl.
2. Crumble 50g / 2oz of the butter into the flour by rubbing it between your fingers. Add 50g / 2oz sugar, a pinch of salt and the yeast and mix thoroughly.
3. Crack two eggs into a bowl. Gently warm the milk in a saucepan, but do not boil.
4. Remove the saucepan from the heat, add the eggs to the milk and stir.
5. Combine the milk and egg mix with the flour, butter, sugar and yeast in the mixing bowl. Stir thoroughly until it forms a dough.
6. On a surface apply a dusting of plain flour. Turn out the dough mix and knead for 10 minutes by hand.
7. Place the dough back in the mixing bowl and cover with cling film. Leave in a warm place until doubled in size. This should take approximately 1 hour.
8. 10 minutes before the dough is ready, place a second saucepan on a low heat and add the remaining butter.

When the butter has melted, add the remaining sugar, the mixed dried fruit and the cinnamon and stir.
9. When the dough is ready, re-dust the surface and roll out to a square. Pour the fruit mix from the saucepan over the square and spread evenly.
10. Dust the baking tray with the plain flour. Roll up the square of dough to form a cylinder. Cut the cylinder into 12 equal slices and lay them out flat on the dusted baking tray. Leave in a warm place until the buns have doubled in size. This should take approximately 1 hour.
11. 10 minutes before the dough has finished rising, pre-heat the oven to 200°C / 400°F / Gas Mark 6.
12. Bake for 30 minutes until golden brown and set aside to cool.
13. For the glaze, heat 4 tablespoons of water in a saucepan and add the icing sugar. Stir and use a pastry brush to apply to each of the buns. Top each bun with a glacé cherry.

LL COOL SOUFFLÉ
Ladies love cool soufflés

DESKTOP

DIFFICULTY

DESCRIPTION
A light and airy chocolatey
dessert served in ramekins.

B.P.M.
10 minutes preparation
25 minutes cooking

INGREDIENTS
4 eggs
50g / 2oz dark chocolate
50g / 2oz milk chocolate
50g / 2oz caster sugar
A small knob of butter
(to grease the ramekins/bowls)
Single cream (to taste)

DESSERTS

METHOD

1. Pre-heat the oven to 150°C /
300°F / Gas Mark 2 and rub the
inside of the ramekins (or bowls)
with butter and set aside.
2. Crack the eggs and separate
the yolks from the whites.*
Discard two of the yolks.
Whisk the other two yolks
gently until they begin to turn
light and set aside. Ensuring
the yolks do not mix with the
egg whites, collect the whites
together into a single bowl.
3. Using a whisk beat the egg
whites into soft peaks.
4. Slowly pour in the sugar
while continuing to whisk the
egg whites. When all the sugar
is added the mix should be
glossy and thick.
5. Fill a saucepan with water
and bring to the boil. Reduce
to a simmer and place the
heatproof mixing bowl over
the water.
6. Add both the milk and dark
chocolate to the heatproof
bowl. Continuously stir the
chocolate mix to ensure it
does not burn and that all
chunks melt.

7. Once the chocolate has
melted, keep it on a low heat
and mix in the two egg yolks
set aside earlier.
8. Stir a tablespoon of the egg
white mix into the chocolate
and yolk mix.
9. Very gently, add the rest
of the egg white mix to the
molten chocolate mix. It is
important to be gentle to
ensure that the air trapped
in the egg white mix does
not escape.
10. Spoon the mix into each of
the four ramekins and smooth
the edges.
11. Place the ramekins onto
the top shelf of the oven for 25
minutes. Do not open the oven
while the soufflés are cooking
or they will collapse.
12. Remove from the oven and
serve with a dollop of the single
cream to taste.

* See *Advanced Methods* p79 for
guidance on separating eggs.

AFRIKA BAMBATTERED PINEAPPLE FRITTERS
& the Soulsonic sauce

DIFFICULTY

DESCRIPTION

Battered pineapple rings
accompanied by a maple
syrup and chilli dipping sauce.

B.P.M.

10 minutes preparation
5 minutes cooking

INGREDIENTS

1 tin of pineapple rings
2 chilli peppers
300ml / half a pint
of maple syrup
120g / 4oz plain flour
2 eggs
150ml / third of a pint of water
1 tablespoon of butter
Icing sugar (to dust)
A pinch of salt
300ml / half a pint of olive oil

METHOD

1. Finely slice the chilli pepper. Place a saucepan on a low heat.
Add the chilli peppers, pour in the maple syrup and mix together.
2. Sift a flour into a mixing bowl and add the salt. Pull the mix to
the sides to form a well in the centre of the bowl.
3. Place a frying pan on medium heat and melt the butter.
4. Boil a kettle for a few seconds (so the water is warmed slightly,
but nowhere near boiling). Pour the warm water into the well in
the mixing bowl. Add the melted butter and stir the mixture to
create a batter. Using a whisk, beat until the batter is smooth.
5. Crack the eggs into the batter and stir thoroughly.
6. Place a second saucepan on a high heat and pour in the olive oil.
7. Using a fork or a skewer pick up a pineapple ring and dip it
into the batter, then gently dip into the hot oil. Hold the battered
pineapple ring in the oil until it is golden and crisp.
8. Place on kitchen paper to dry and then dust with icing sugar.
9. Serve on a plate and pour over the maple and chilli sauce.

MOUSSE DEF

Feat. Talib Jelly

DESSERTS

DIFFICULTY

DESCRIPTION

A thick, rich chocolate mousse
served with fruit jelly and
topped with fresh berries.

B.P.M.

20 minutes mousse
preparation
1 hour mousse setting
15 minutes jelly preparation
45 minutes jelly setting

INGREDIENTS

4 eggs
400g /14oz dark chocolate
150g / 5oz unsalted butter
4 gelatine leaves
100g / 4oz raspberries
100g / 4oz strawberries
100g / 4oz blueberries
500ml / 1 pint
of cranberry juice
3 tablespoons of water

METHOD

For the Mousse Def

1. Crack the eggs and separate
the yolks from the whites into
two separate bowls*.
2. Using a whisk, beat the egg
whites into soft peaks.
3. Slice the butter into chunks
and set aside.
4. Fill a saucepan with water
and bring to the boil. Reduce
to a simmer and place the
heatproof mixing bowl over
the water. Add the chocolate
and butter chunks and stir
continuously.
5. Once the chocolate has
melted, remove the bowl from
the heat and mix in the egg
yolks. Leave this mixture to cool
for 5 minutes.
6. Fold the egg whites into
the chocolate, butter and yolk
mixture. Divide the mixture
between four of the ramekins.
Cover each ramekin with
clingfilm and leave to cool in the
fridge for 1 hour.

* See *Advanced Methods* p79 for
guidance on separating eggs.

For the Talib Jelly

1. Place the gelatine leaves
in a bowl and cover with cold
water to soften.
2. Wash the strawberries,
blueberries and raspberries
under cold water. Slice the
strawberries and add to a
mixing bowl with the other
berries. Separate out into four
ramekins or serving bowls.
3. Boil a kettle of water.
Place the softened gelatine
leaves into a measuring jug
and pour 3 tablespoons of
boiling water over them.
Mix the gelatine leaves and
the hot water to dissolve the
gelatine. Add the cranberry
juice to the dissolved gelatine
and stir.
4. Pour the jelly into each of
the ramekins over the fruit,
which we divided between
the four ramekins or serving
bowls and place in the fridge
for 45 minutes.
5. When serving, give each
person a ramekin of jelly and
a ramekin of juice.

THE SUGAR HILL MERINGUE
The original Rapper's Delight

DESSERTS

DIFFICULTY

DESCRIPTION

Tasty nests of meringue
flavoured with vanilla, rose
water and dill.

B.P.M.

30 minutes preparation
1 – 2 hours cooking

INGREDIENTS

4 eggs
215g / 8oz caster sugar
2 teaspoons of cornflour
1 teaspoon of rosewater essence
1 teaspoon of white vinegar
2 vanilla pods
2 sprigs of dill
2 ice cubes
3 drops of pink food colouring
(optional)

NOTES

If you can't get vanilla pods,
you can use 3 drops of vanilla
essence instead. This recipe
is difficult to make if you don't
have an electric whisk.

METHOD

1. Pre-heat the oven to 110°C /
225°F / Gas Mark one quarter.
2. Line a baking tray with
baking paper.
3. Slice the stalk from the vanilla
pods and carefully slice down
the length of the pod. Using a
spoon scrape out the seeds from
the pod and set aside.
4. Add the dill, vanilla pods,
rose water, white wine vinegar,
food colouring and ice cubes
to the cocktail shaker. Shake
vigorously for 1 minute.
5. Separate the egg yolks from
the 4 eggs*, setting aside the
yolks and whites in separate
bowls. Ensure no yolk has
mixed with the egg whites.
Transfer the whites into a
mixing bowl.
6. Using an electric whisk (or
manual whisk), beat the egg
whites into soft peaks.
7. Continue to whisk and add
the caster sugar one tablespoon
at a time. Continue beating for 2
seconds between each addition.
When all the caster sugar is
added the mixture should be
thick, smooth and shiny.

8. Add the vanilla seeds
and pour the liquid from the
cocktail shaker through a
sieve, discarding any solids.
Gently fold the mix for a
few seconds.
9. Spoon the mixture onto the
baking paper-covered tray in
four equal sized mounds.
10. Bake in the oven for 1 hour
and 20 minutes, or until the
meringues are crisp and pale
in colour. This may take up
to an additional 40 minutes
depending on your oven.
11. Leave to cool for 15
minutes before serving.

* See *Advanced Methods* p79 for
guidance on separating eggs.

ADVANCED

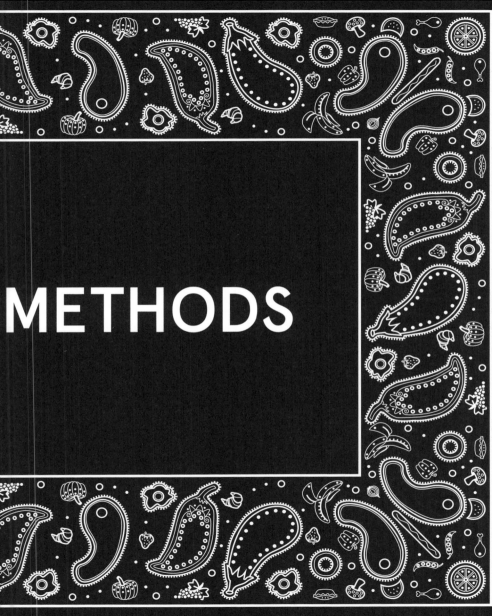

METHODS

ADVANCED METHODS
Playas only

ADVANCED METHOD 1: POACHING EGGS – POACHING A SINGLE EGG

FEATURED IN
DM Eggs Benedict

INGREDIENTS
Egg(s)
1 tablespoon of vinegar
A pinch of salt

EQUIPMENT
Saucepan
Cup
Wooden spoon
Slotted spoon

METHOD

1. Place a saucepan on a high heat, fill with water and bring to the boil.
2. Reduce the heat to a rolling simmer and add the salt and vinegar.
3. Carefully crack the egg into a cup, ensuring no fragments of shell fall in.
4. Swirl the water around in the saucepan to create a slight whirlpool effect.
5. Gently pour the egg from the cup into the centre of the whirlpool in the saucepan.
6. After 3 minutes use an slotted spoon to gently remove the egg from the saucepan.

ADVANCED METHOD 2: POACHING EGGS – USING AN EGG POACHER

FEATURED IN
DM Eggs Benedict

INGREDIENTS
Egg(s)
1 tablespoon of vinegar
1 drop of olive oil (per egg)

EQUIPMENT
Saucepan
Egg poacher(s)

METHOD

1. Place a saucepan on a high heat, fill with water and bring to the boil.
2. Reduce the heat to a low simmer and add the vinegar.
3. Add a drop of the olive oil and use your fingers to grease the inside of the egg poacher.
4. Carefully crack an egg into the egg poacher, being sure that no fragments of shell have fallen in.
5. Gently place the egg poacher onto surface of the water in the centre of the saucepan.
6. After 6 minutes carefully remove the egg from the saucepan.

ADVANCED METHOD 3: POACHING EGGS - WRAPPED POACHING METHOD

FEATURED IN

DM Eggs Benedict

INGREDIENTS

Egg(s)

1 tablespoon of vinegar

EQUIPMENT

Saucepan

Cup

Wooden spoon

Cling film

Bull clip / heat-resistant bag clip

Scissors

Slotted spoon

METHOD

1. Cut a 20cm by 20cm (14" by 14") square from the cling film. Lay this over the cup and push the cling film into the cup to create a pouch.

2. Carefully crack an egg into this pouch, ensuring no fragments of shell fall in.

3. Bring the edges of the cling film up, wrapping around the egg. Twist the cling film to create a ball encasing the egg. Try to ensure no air is caught in with the egg.

4. Use the clip to fasten the twisted tail of cling film and cut off any excess cling film.

5. Place a saucepan on a high heat, fill with water and bring to the boil.

6. After 6 minutes use an egg spoon to gently remove the egg from the saucepan.

7. Gently place the wrapped egg in the saucepan.

8. After 3 minutes use an slotted spoon to gently remove the egg from the saucepan.

ADVANCED METHOD 4: SEPARATING AN EGG

FEATURED IN

DM Eggs Benedict

Busta Key Lime Pie

LL Cool Soufflé

Mousse Def

The Sugar Hill Meringue

INGREDIENTS

Egg(s)

EQUIPMENT

2 cups

METHOD

1. Being careful not to break the egg yolk, crack an egg into one of the cups.

2. Pour the egg from the first cup into the second using the top edge of the empty cup to trap the egg yolk.

3. The egg yolk should remain in the first cup while the egg white falls into the second cup.

ADVANCED METHOD 5: GANGSTARTAR SAUCE

FEATURED IN
Lemon Sole of Mischief

DESCRIPTION
Traditional tartar sauce to
accompany any fish dish.

B.P.M.
5 minutes preparation

INGREDIENTS
8 tablespoons of mayonnaise
2 tablespoons of capers
2 tablespoons of pickled gherkins
1 sprig of parsley
1 lemon
A pinch of salt
A pinch of black pepper

EQUIPMENT
Colander
Chopping board
Mixing bowl
Wooden spoon

METHOD

1. Drain and finely slice the capers, gherkins (aka pickled
cucumbers) and parsley.
2. Add the mayonnaise, capers, gherkins and parsley to a
mixing bowl and stir vigorously.
3. Slice the lemon in half and squeeze the juice into the
mixing bowl.
4. Add the salt and pepper and give the mix a final stir.

ADVANCED METHOD 6: ACCOMPANYING VEGETABLES

DESCRIPTION
Cooking times for your
accompanying vegetables.

EQUIPMENT
Saucepan
Wooden spoon
Colander

METHOD

Refer to chart on opposite page for separate cooking times.

1. Place a saucepan on a high heat, fill with water and bring to
the boil.
2. Reduce the heat to a simmer and add a pinch of salt.
3. Add the vegetables and cook for the required time.
4. Drain the vegetables through the colander.

COOKING TIMES FOR ACCOMPANYING VEGETABLES

	0 mins	5 mins	10 mins	15 mins	20 mins	25 mins
Peas						
Broccoli						
Corn on the cob						
Cauliflower						
Brussel sprouts						
Runner beans						
Leeks						
New potatoes						
Carrots						
Spinach						
Asparagus						
Turnip						

ADVANCED METHODS

ADVANCED METHOD 7: COLCANNON MASH

FEATURED IN
Queen Labeefah

DESCRIPTION
Traditional Irish
creamy potatoes.

B.P.M.
5 minutes preparation
20 minutes cooking

INGREDIENTS
700g / 25oz potatoes
200g / 7oz cabbage
A bunch of spring onions
(approx. 100g / 4oz)
50g / 2oz butter
150ml / quarter of a pint
of single cream
A pinch of salt
A pinch of black pepper

EQUIPMENT
Chopping board
Peeler
Masher
Wooden spoon
Frying pan
Saucepan

METHOD

1. Finely slice the cabbage and the spring onions, discard the routes, and set aside. Peel and slice the potatoes into 1 inch / 2.5 cm cubes.
2. Place a saucepan on a high heat and fill with water. Bring to the boil, add a pinch of salt and reduce to a simmer. Add the potatoes to the saucepan. After 15 minutes remove the saucepan from the heat.
3. Place a frying pan on a medium heat and add the butter. When the butter has melted, add the cabbage and spring onions. Stir the mix in the frying pan occasionally for 3 minutes.
4. Using a colander, drain the water from the potatoes. Return the potatoes to the saucepan and crush with the masher.
5. Add the cooked cabbage, spring onions and cream to the saucepan and thoroughly stir with the wooden spoon. Season with black pepper.

ADVANCED METHOD 8: CREAMED LEEKS

FEATURED IN
Queen Labeefah

DESCRIPTION
A perfect creamy
accompaniment for a wide
range of meals.

B.P.M.
4 minutes preparation
20 minutes cooking

INGREDIENTS
50g / 2oz butter
100ml / one fifth of a pint
of dry white wine
150ml / quarter of a pint of
single cream
4 leeks

EQUIPMENT
Saucepan
Chopping board
Wooden spoon

METHOD

1. Wash and finely slice the leeks.
2. Place a saucepan on a medium heat. Add the butter to the saucepan.
3. After 1 minute add the leeks, stirring occasionally.
4. After 15 minutes, add the wine to the saucepan and stir thoroughly.
5. Continuously stirring the mix, add the cream.
6. Cook for 2 minutes before seasoning with a pinch of salt.

ADVANCED METHOD 9: SLOW COOKING – OLD SCHOOL STYLE

FEATURED IN
Pig Bun

NOTES
While purpose-made slow cookers are very convenient, the art of slow cooking meats has been around since way back in the yesteryears. The following methods can be used as alternatives to the use of an electric slow cooker.

EQUIPMENT
Method 1:
Saucepan with lid
Method 2:
Barbecue with lid
Saucepan or cooking pot
Method 3:
Small oven-safe dish
Large oven-safe dish with lid

METHOD 1: IN A POT

1. Place a saucepan on a high heat, fill with water and bring to the boil.
2. Reduce the heat to its lowest setting and add your ingredients.
3. Cover with a lid and cook for the required time.
4. While cooking, check periodically to ensure the water level continues to cover the meat.

METHOD 2: OVER A BARBECUE

1. Heat your barbecue and place the saucepan or cooking pot in the centre.
2. Add your ingredients and close the barbecue lid.
3. Cook for the required time.
4. While cooking, check periodically to ensure the water level continues to cover the meat.
5. If the barbecue runs out of fuel, you can carefully bring the saucepan or cooking pot inside and finish cooking on your hob.
6. The food will absorb the barbecue flavours as it cooks.

METHOD 3: SMOKE IT UP

1. Place a small oven-safe dish in a larger oven-safe dish and fill the void with the smoking material.
2. Add your ingredients to the smaller dish and top up with water. Put the lid over the larger dish.
3. Turn your oven on at a low heat and place the dishes in the centre.
4. Cook for the required time.
5. While cooking, check periodically to ensure the water level continues to cover the meat and that the smoking material has not dried out or ignited.
6. The food will absorb the flavours of the smoke as it cooks.

ADVANCED METHOD 10: HOMEMADE CUSTARD

FEATURED IN

Nasty na'Nas & Custard

DESCRIPTION

A sweet sauce made from
cream, eggs and sugar.

B.P.M.

5 minutes preparation
15 minutes cooking

INGREDIENTS

1 vanilla pod
500ml / 1 pint of double cream
1 tablespoon icing sugar
6 large eggs
125g / 4 and a half oz
caster sugar
1 tablespoon of cornflour

EQUIPMENT

Chopping board
Wooden spoon
2 Saucepans
Whisk
Tongs

METHOD

1. Place the vanilla pod on a chopping board. Using the tip of
a sharp knife, slice down the vanilla pod and, using a spoon,
scrape out the seeds.

2. Add the eggs, caster sugar, icing sugar and cornflour to a
mixing bowl and whisk for 3 minutes.

3. Place a saucepan on a low heat and add the cream and vanilla.
Using the wooden spoon stir for 2 minutes.

4. One tablespoon at a time, add the hot vanilla cream to the
eggs, whisking continually.

5. Place a clean saucepan on a low heat and pour in the mix.
Stir with a wooden spoon for 12 minutes and take off the heat.

6. To serve, use the tongs to remove the vanilla pod and pour the
custard into a serving jug.

EXTEND

RECIPE INDEX
Starters

12
PUBLIC ENEMISO SOUP
by Hattie Stewart
hattiestewart.com
Difficulty: 1/5
B.P.M: 5m prep 10m cooking

14
WU-TANG CLAM CHOWDE
by Andy Baker
andy-baker.com
Difficulty: 5/5
B.P.M: 25m prep 45m cooking

22
DM EGGS BENEDICT
by Matt Robinson
wrigglesandrobins.com
Difficulty: 4/5
B.P.M: 15m prep 30m cooking

24
MC HAM'N'EGGS
by Joe Bichard
joebichard.com
Difficulty: 3/5
B.P.M: 2m prep 18m cooking

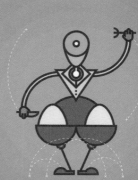

16
HOBB LEEK & POTATO SOUP
by Misterlego
misterlego.com
Difficulty: 2/5
B.P.M: 10m prep 15m cooking

18
MC SOLAARIAC SOUP
by Mudrok
samuelmurdoch.co.uk
Difficulty: 3/5
B.P.M: 5m prep 25m cooking

20
PRAWN CARTER COCKTAIL
by Alice Hartley
alicehartley.co.uk
Difficulty: 2/5
B.P.M: 5m prep 4m cooking

26
LUDACRISPY DUCK
by Adam Cruft
adamcruft.com
Difficulty: 2/5
B.P.M: 10m prep 6m cooking

28
METHOD LAMB KOFTAS
by Emily Frances Barrett
emilyfrancesbarrett.com
Difficulty: 2/5
B.P.M: 5m prep 10m cooking

30
MF SHROOM BURGERS
by Tom J Newell
tomjnewell.com
Difficulty: 2/5
B.P.M: 15m prep 15m cooking

RECIPE INDEX
Mains

34
NOTORIOUS P.I.G.
by Bradley Jay
bradleyjay.co.uk
Difficulty: 3/5
B.P.M: 10m prep 15m cooking

36
RUN DM SEA BASS
by Yu Sato
yousato.com
Difficulty: 2/5
B.P.M: 5m prep 25m cooking

44
SLICK RICOTTA TART
by Peter Stadden
peterstadden.co.uk
Difficulty: 2/5
B.P.M: 20m prep 20m cooking

46
QUEEN LABEEFAH
by Cassie Agazzi Brooks
cassiebrooks.co.uk
Difficulty: 5/5
B.P.M: 30m prep 30m cooking

38
ANDMASTER FLASH FRIED STEAK
by Maggie Li
maggie.li
Difficulty: 3/5
B.P.M: 20m prep 5m cooking

40
LEMON SOLE OF MISCHIEF
by Anna Brooks
anna-brooks.com
Difficulty: 3/5
B.P.M: 15m prep 50m cooking

42
SNOOP STROGANOFF
by J W Luxton
wearebuild.com
Difficulty: 4/5
B.P.M: 1h15 prep 25m cooking

48
PIG BUN
by Patch D Keyes
patchdkeyes.co.uk
Difficulty: 4/5
B.P.M: 10m prep 8h cooking

50
A PIE CALLED QUEST
by Jason Munro
jason-munro.co.uk
Difficulty: 3/5
B.P.M: 15m prep 1h20m cooking

52
N.W. GLAZED HAM
by Tom Bunker
cargocollective.com/tombunker
Difficulty: 4/5
B.P.M: 10m prep 3h30m cooking

RECIPE INDEX Desserts

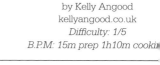

56
EAZY ETON MESS
by Bart
illustrator-bart.co.uk
Difficulty: 1/5
B.P.M: 15m prep 5m cooking

58
M.O.PEACH COBBLER
by Kelly Angood
kellyangood.co.uk
Difficulty: 1/5
B.P.M: 15m prep 1h10m cooki

66
KRS BUNS
by Daniel Boyle
treatstudios.com
Difficulty: 3/5
B.P.M: 15m prep 2h cooking

68
LL COOL SOUFFLÉS
by Jack Cunningham
jack-cunningham.tumblr.com
Difficulty: 5/5
B.P.M: 10m prep 25m cooking

60
NASTY NA'NAS & CUSTARD
by Paul Hill
iamvagabond.co.uk
Difficulty: 3/5
B.P.M: 5m prep 15m cooking

62
BUSTA KEY LIME PIE
by Lynnie Zulu
lynniezulu.com
Difficulty: 4/5
B.P.M: 15m prep 25m cooking

64
TIRAMISU ELLIOTT
by Yeji Yun
seeouterspace.com
Difficulty: 5/5
B.P.M: 30m prep 6h cooling

70
RIKA BAMBATTERED P. FRITTERS
by Paul Layzell
paul-layzell.com
Difficulty: 2/5
B.P.M: 10m prep 5m cooking

72
MOUSSE DEF
by Tom Edwards
edwardstom.com
Difficulty: 3/5
B.P.M: 20m prep 1h setting

74
SUGAR HILL MERINGUE
by Suzi Kemp
suzikemp.com
Difficulty: 5/5
B.P.M: 30m prep 1-2h cooking

RAPPER'S DELIGHT MIXTAPE

The definitive collection of beats to cook to

Cooking just isn't the same without beats. In the official *Rapper's Delight* mixtape, every one of the thirty recipes is catered for. For the full *Rapper's Delight* experience, scan the QR code or visit www.rappersdelightcookbook.com. Warning: some lyrics are explicit.

1. Public Enemy – Don't Believe The Hype
2. Wu-Tang Clan – Triumph
3. Mobb Deep – Survival Of The Fittest
4. MC Solaar – Nouveau Western
5. Jay-Z & Kanye West – Ni**as In Paris
6. DMX - Party Up (Up In Here)
7. MC Hammer – U Can't Touch This
8. Ludacris – Roll Out
9. Wu-Tang Clan – Method Man
10. MF DOOM – Hoe Cakes

11. Notorious B.I.G. – Hypnotize
12. Run DMC – It's Tricky
13. Grandmaster Flash & The Furious Five – The Message
14. Souls of Mischief – Cab Fare
15. Snoop Dogg – Who Am I (What's My Name)

16. Slick Rick & Doug E Fresh – La Di Da Di
17. Queen Latifah & Monie Love – Ladies First
18. Big Pun Feat. Fat Joe – Twinz (98 Deep Cover)
19. A Tribe Called Quest – Electric Relaxation
20. N.W.A. – Straight Outta Compton

21. Eazy-E – Eazy Duz It
22. M.O.P. Feat. Busta Rhymes – Ante Up
23. Nas – Made You Look
24. Busta Rhymes – Dangerous
25. Missy Elliott – Get Ur Freak On
26. KRS One – MC's Act Like They Don't Know
27. LL Cool J – Going Back To Cali
28. Afrika Bambaataa & Soulsonic Force – Planet Rock
29. Black Star – Definition
30. The Sugarhill Gang – Rapper's Delight

OUTRO

Peas to all of our culinary brothers and sisters...

We'd like to say thanks to the following people for their support and contribution to the making of *Rapper's Delight* cookbook:

Björn Almqvist and the team at Dokument Press, Adam Cruft, Alice Hartley, Andy Baker, Anna Brooks, Bradley Jay, Cassie Agazzi Brooks, Daniel Boyle, Emily Frances Barrett, Fran Carson, Gabriele Rizzetto, Hattie Stewart, Jack Cunningham, James Reynolds, Jamie Rio, Jason Munro, Joe Bichard, Joe Luxton, Katie Baxter, Kelly Angood, Lynnie Zulu, Maggie Li, Misterlego, Paul Hill, Patch D Keyes, Patrick Dishman, Paul Layzell, Penny Miller, Peter Miller, Rebecca Morris, Rob Hastings, Rona Inniss, Sam Murdoch, Susan Inniss, Suzi Kemp, Tom Brown, Tom Bunker, Tom Clohosy Cole, Tom Edwards, Tom J Newell, Vicki Murphy, Will Finlay, Wriggles and Robins, Yeji Yun, Yu Sato.

Finally, a special mention for Ralph Miller's artistic efforts, which unfortunately didn't quite make the cut.

Will.i.ham sandwich by Ralph Miller (aged 27 ½)

Rapper's Delight community

If you enjoyed this book, had any comments or other recipe ideas, we'd love to hear from you.

 www.rappersdelightcookbook.com

 facebook.com/rappersdelightcookbook

 @rapperscookbook

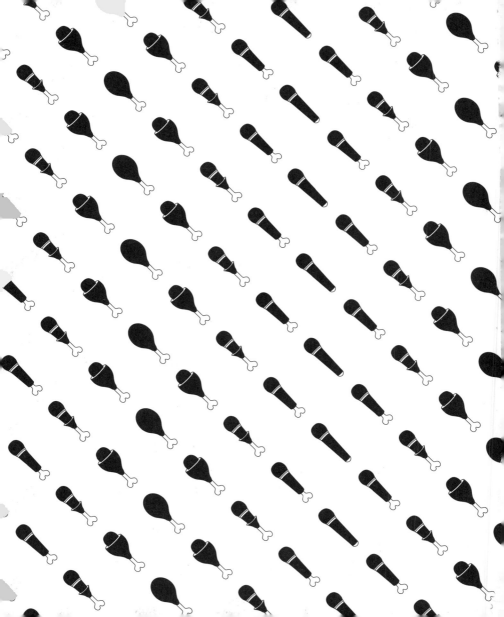